garlic

By JANET HAZEN

Illustrated by Dorothy Reinhardt

Chronicle Books • San Francisco

Printed in Hong Kong.

Library of Congress-Cataloging-in Publication Data
Hazen, Janet.
  Garlic / by Janet Hazen : illustrated by Dorothy Reinhardt.
    p.   cm.
  ISBN 0-8118-0197-7 (hardcover)
  1. Cookery (Garlic)   I. Title.
  TX819.G3H39   1992
  641.6'526–dc20   92-2556
                                                                    CIP

Editing: Carolyn Krebs
Book and cover design: Merrick Hamilton

Distributed in Canada by Raincoast Books, 112 East Third Ave.,
Vancouver, B.C. V5T 1C8

10 9 8 7 6 5 4 3 2

Chronicle Books
275 Fifth Street
San Francisco, CA 94103

CONTENTS

introduction

FEW FOODS HAVE ELICITED MORE PASSION and controversy than garlic. Historically, garlic has played a powerful role in the culinary, medicinal, and religious practices of many cultures. Ancient Greeks, Indians, Chinese, and Egyptians all used garlic in a variety of ways. For example, garlic was given to Egyptian slaves to build their strength while constructing the Pyramids. Records show that the Chinese used garlic both in cooking and as a medicine over four thousand years ago. Mesopotamian tablets dating from 1700 B.C. contained collections of culinary recipes featuring garlic.

Much of our historical fascination with garlic comes from a belief in its magical and healing attributes. The mystical powers ascribed to the bulb in almost every part of the world include the ability to ward off vampires and evil spirits. During the 1700s, peasants in central Europe hung strands of garlic on their front doors to protect themselves against evil; Hindus in India used it to fight demons. As a folk remedy, garlic has been used as a cure for high blood pressure and for combating colds, flu, arthritis, rheumatism, bronchial disorders, cancer, and internal infections. Ancient Egyptians used it to cure toothaches and consumption and to heal wounds.

The English word *garlic* comes from the Anglo-Saxon word *garleac,* for "spear leek." Garlic is a member of the genus *Allium*, which includes leeks, onions, chives, and shallots. Its head, consisting of indi-

vidual cloves, grows underground and sends up erect green shoots. Each fleshy clove is encased in a thin, papery skin, and the whole bulb is wrapped in several layers of slightly thicker skin the color of parchment. The cloves and the green shoots are edible in both raw and cooked form.

For centuries, garlic has appeared with regularity in recipes from Asia to the Mediterranean to South and Central America, but it wasn't until the late 1960s that North Americans embraced garlic with any kind of fervor. Like the English, Americans considered garlic offensive in both flavor and odor and avoided dishes that included the ingredient. Secret garlic lovers who emitted any trace of garlic aroma were regarded as social misfits.

More adventurous American cooks of the 1950s would occasionally use powdered garlic or garlic salt—both greatly inferior to the fresh bulb. Although a small percentage of the population used garlic for its health benefits, most cooks didn't know that garlic was a fresh food ingredient until they sampled ethnic cuisines and developed an interest in cooking these exotic foods for themselves.

The current trend towards healthful eating and low-fat cooking makes fresh garlic an essential ingredient in today's diet. When combined with fresh lemon, lime, or vinegar, garlic can bring out the natu-

ral flavors in food, thus alleviating the need for unwanted salt.

It is rare to sample a well-prepared dish and feel there is an excessive amount of garlic in it, but when garlic is missing, the absence can be glaring and disappointing. Rubbed on toasted bread, with a little olive oil, garlic can elevate a common snack to the sublime. Sautéed in olive oil and combined with fresh tomatoes and herbs, garlic forms the basis for a terrific, healthy, and simple pasta dish. Chicken and rice soup perfumed with fresh garlic makes a heavenly cure for the common cold. Pizza topped with fresh garlic and clams could improve anyone's dark mood.

Today, Americans are interested in more than just the health aspects of cooking and eating; we are fascinated with robust and complex flavors. We have been introduced to the pleasures of cooking international foods that include garlic as a staple ingredient. Garlic has become the ultimate comfort food—its incomparable smell and flavor provide nourishment for the heart and soul, as well as the body. When the inviting fragrance of garlic is present, we immediately associate it with good food. Cooking without garlic would be like painting without color; it is a source of inspiration to those who cook and share food with friends and family. With garlic we can create wonderful, tempting dishes that will make lasting impressions, whatever the occasion.

A GARLIC COMPENDIUM

PURCHASING GARLIC. Garlic is available year-round because it is grown and harvested in all corners of the world. Much of the garlic sold in the United States is grown in California; it is also imported to the United States from Mexico and Chile.

When purchasing garlic, look for heads that are dry, hard, and generously covered by a thin, papery outer skin. Garlic heads that are sprouting green shoots are past their prime, and quite possibly weren't dried properly. Heads with larger cloves are easier to peel and handle, but heads with smaller cloves are fine for cooking as well.

Elephant garlic, an *Allium* related to garlic, has cloves several times larger than those of ordinary garlic. Elephant garlic has a milder, subtler flavor; therefore, the two are not interchangeable in recipes. Elephant garlic can be found in the produce department near the garlic and onions in most grocery stores. Specialty produce markets, natural food stores, and farmers' markets also carry elephant garlic. It is sold by the head (usually wrapped in plastic netting), or by the individual clove, priced per pound. Purchasing guidelines are the same as for ordinary garlic.

STORING GARLIC. Fresh garlic, stored in a cool, dry place, will keep for several months. If stored in a container that allows air to circulate around the bulbs, it will last even longer. I have successfully kept garlic for months at a cool, dry room temperature and prefer this method of storage over refrigeration, which can make the garlic soft and wet if kept for a long period of time. Some people like to use a hanging basket to store their garlic, others prefer to store it in bowls or garlic pots, and some are able to buy large braids of fresh garlic from which they can pluck a whole head whenever needed.

PREPARING GARLIC.

Head versus clove: The large bulb of individual cloves encased in a thin, white, papery covering is referred to as the *head*. The small, individual bulbs within the head are called *cloves*. Some people refer to a clove as a *tooth* of garlic, but in this book I use the term *clove*.

To separate whole cloves from the head: Place the head of garlic, root side down, on a flat cutting surface. Using a flat, heavy object, such as a cast-iron skillet, firmly press down on the top of the head, forcing the cloves to disengage from the root and center stem. Loosen the cloves from the root end and from the center stem.

To peel cloves of garlic that will be minced or chopped: Place the clove on a flat cutting board; using the broad side of a large kitchen knife, smash the clove so that the skin breaks away from the flesh. Remove and discard the skin. The garlic is now ready for mincing or chopping.

To peel cloves of garlic that will be sliced or left whole: Remove the skin with a small paring knife or with your fingers. It is helpful to remove the small brown "nub" at the bottom of the clove, where the skin is attached to the root.

To peel several heads of garlic at once: Separate the cloves and drop into boiling water for 1 minute, then drain and cool. The skins will slip off. The disadvantage to this method is that the garlic cooks slightly and loses some of its flavor.

TO MINCE OR TO CHOP? The choice of whether to press, mince, chop, or slice garlic cloves is dictated by the type of dish being prepared, the length of cooking time, and the strength of garlic flavor desired. In general, the smaller the "cut," the more pronounced the garlic flavor and the more rapidly it blends with other ingredients in a dish. For this reason, I use the small cuts—pressed or minced—in recipes that require little or no cooking, such as vinaigrettes and salads; or in dishes with delicate textures and flavors where larger chunks of garlic would be inappropriate. The larger cuts—chopped, sliced, or even whole cloves—are used in more rustic dishes that will be cooked for longer periods of time; when it will be puréed later in a blender; or when a less pronounced flavor is desired.

To press or crush garlic: Peel the clove and place in a garlic press; force the pulp through the small holes of the press using the handle and pressing mechanism. It is important to buy a heavy, strong garlic press, preferably one with a flexible pressing mechanism.

To mince garlic: Peel the clove and flatten with the blade of a large kitchen knife. Cut the clove into very tiny pieces.

To chop garlic: Peel the clove and cut into small pieces with a sharp kitchen knife. Finely chopped garlic is slightly larger than minced, and coarsely chopped garlic is slightly larger still. Garlic also can be chopped in a food processor using the on and off switch to pulse the garlic until the desired size is achieved.

To slice garlic: Peel the clove and lay on a flat cutting surface. With a very sharp knife, slice lengthwise into thin pieces.

TO FRY OR SAUTÉ? As with cutting garlic, the method chosen to cook garlic is dictated by the type of dish being prepared, the strength of garlic flavor desired, the other cooking methods in the recipe, and the final appearance of the dish.

Fried garlic is cooked in hot oil at a much higher temperature and for a shorter period of time than when it is sautéed, yielding crisp, thoroughly cooked garlic with a golden brown color. Fried garlic has a crunchy texture and a sweet, nutty flavor. To preserve its texture, it is often added to a recipe just before serving or used as a garnish.

Poaching is an excellent method for cooking garlic when the cloves are to remain whole and when a smooth texture and off-white color are desired. Depending on the length of cooking time, the poached cloves can be meltingly soft, firm and dense, or hard and barely cooked. This fat-free cooking method produces garlic that ranges in flavor from mild to bitingly sharp, and can be used for pasta and vegetable dishes or salads.

Roasting in the oven is a popular method of cooking garlic because it renders the finished product sweet, yet full-flavored and silky smooth. Roasted garlic can be used in soups, dressings, dips, pasta dishes, and sauces, or simply spread on toasted bread and served warm. Roasted garlic makes a terrific, fat-free thickening agent for soups, stews, casseroles, or dressings.

Sautéing garlic in hot oil or butter in a skillet or sauté pan is by far the most versatile method of cooking garlic and the most commonly used. Garlic is often sautéed with onions and spices or herbs in the first steps of a recipe to form a savory flavor base for the other ingredients.

To fry garlic: Use a heavy-bottomed saucepan or deep-sided sauté pan for frying. Heat the oil until very hot, but not smoking, about 360° F. Add the peeled cloves of garlic and watch closely. When garlic is fried too fast or browned too much it becomes bitter. Once garlic starts to brown, it tends to burn rather quickly, so it is important to watch the pan carefully if you are frying garlic in oil over moderately high or high heat. Stirring constantly will help prevent the garlic from burning, but once it starts to turn medium-brown, you should remove it from the heat and drain on paper towels.

To poach garlic: Separate the head into cloves; there is no need to peel the individual cloves before poaching because this cooking method will separate the skins from the flesh. Place the separated cloves and the cooking liquid—usually water or wine—in a saucepan. Bring to a boil over high heat, reduce the heat to moderate and cook until soft, about 30 minutes to 1 hour, depending on how big the cloves are and how you intend to use them. If you want to retain the shape of the cloves and serve them whole, cook them until they are tender, but still firm. If the poached cloves will be puréed or mixed into other food, poach them until they are very soft.

To roast whole heads of garlic: Cut a 1/4-inch slice across the top of the whole head so that just the tips of flesh from each individual clove are exposed. Remove the very outer layers of skin. Place, cut side down, in a lightly greased baking dish; fill with water about 2 inches deep. Bake in a preheated 450° F. oven for 50 minutes to 1 hour or until soft; remove from the oven and cool. When cool enough to handle, take the head of garlic in one hand and, holding it as far up around the round root end as possible, squeeze the pulp from the open ends of the cloves; the pulp should come right out, but take care to remove any skin that comes along with it. The roasted garlic pulp is now ready to use in any recipe.

You may roast several heads of garlic at a time and store in the refrigerator for up to 5 days: Place the roasted heads in a small dish and cover with olive oil; cover tightly and refrigerate. Remove the cloves as needed, and use the roasted garlic-flavored oil in dressings and vinaigrettes or for drizzling over vegetables, potatoes, or toasted bread. You may also purée the roasted cloves in a food processor, making a smooth paste to use in soups, dips, and dressings or for spreading on crackers and bread. If serving roasted garlic as an appetizer, it is best to roast and serve the heads whole—each diner can squeeze the garlic from the skins and spread the purée onto bread, croutons, or crackers.

To roast individual cloves: Separate an entire head of garlic and place the unpeeled cloves in a lightly greased baking pan. Bake at 400° F. for 1 hour or until the cloves are soft. Garlic roasted in this manner is usually presented as is; the disadvantage is that each diner must remove the skin from his or her mouth after sucking the roasted garlic from the interior. Individual cloves of garlic are often roasted along with potatoes, vegetables, meat, fish, or poultry, acting as a flavoring agent rather than as a primary ingredient.

To sauté garlic: Use a heavy-bottomed sauté pan or skillet for sautéing, preferably non-stick. Heat the oil or butter first, over moderately high or high heat, then add the garlic. Stir constantly to keep the garlic from burning. Many recipes in this book call for garlic and onions to be sautéed together; since onions cook more slowly than minced or chopped garlic, care must be taken to prevent the garlic from burning before the onion is sufficiently cooked. It is crucial to watch the pan carefully and stir frequently if sautéing garlic with onions in oil over moderately high heat.

An important guideline for sautéing garlic: Butter burns at a much lower temperature than olive oil, so for this reason—and many others—I prefer using a good-quality olive oil for most cooking. Sesame oil, used on occasion in Asian dishes, also has a low burning point so it is usually combined with peanut oil, which has a high burning point.

APPETIZERS

sake-steamed mussels

WITH GARLIC *and* GINGER

Asian ingredients highlight the wonderful texture and flavor of mussels in this simple appetizer. Served with a green salad and warm bread, this shellfish dish makes a warm and inviting supper.

3 pounds fresh mussels (be sure the shells are closed when you buy the mussels)
3 cups sake (Japanese-style rice wine)
2 heads garlic, cloves separated and minced
3-inch piece ginger root, peeled and minced
1 tablespoon ground coriander
2 teaspoons coarsely ground black pepper

Makes 4 servings.

California produces over 90 percent of the 150 million pounds of garlic grown each year in the United States.

Scrub the mussels with a stiff brush, removing the beards and any sand or grit. Soak in cold water for 1 hour and drain before cooking.

Place the sake, garlic, ginger, coriander, and black pepper in a very large, shallow saucepan. Bring to a boil over high heat and cook for 5 minutes, stirring frequently. Add the mussels and return to a boil. Reduce the heat to moderate, cover, and cook for 4 to 6 minutes or until most of the mussels have opened. Remove the opened mussels and place in a serving bowl. Cover and cook the remaining mussels for 2 minutes. Add the opened mussels to the serving bowl, discarding any unopened mussels. Spoon the cooking liquid over the mussels, and serve at once.

mediterranean garlic-hot pepper olives

It is best to use imported Greek or Italian olives for this feisty hors d'oeuvre, but even ordinary black olives will be greatly improved by the spicy marinade. These olives are better if served at least one week after marinating, and they continue to improve with age, up to one month.

1 cup extra-virgin olive oil
1/2 cup red wine vinegar
12 cloves garlic, thinly sliced
1 tablespoon fennel seeds
1 to 2 teaspoons hot pepper flakes
Grated zest from 1 orange
2 1/2 cups Kalamata, oil-cured,
  or ripe green olives

Makes about 8 servings.

Combine the olive oil, vinegar, fennel seeds, hot pepper flakes, and orange zest in a large bowl; mix well. Add the ol-ives and let stand at room temperature for 2 hours, stirring from time to time. Serve the drained olives at room temperature, or cover, undrained, and refrigerate up to 1 month.

skordalia

GREEK GARLIC *and* POTATO PURÉE

A simpler version of this classic Greek dish is made with stale bread, but I think this recipe is interesting because the potatoes give it a more substantial texture and flavor. *Skordalia* is often served with wild greens, beets, and deep-fried cod or shark; or with bread, olives, *dolmas*, raw vegetables, and grilled lamb or chicken.

4 large baking potatoes (about 2 pounds)
8 cloves garlic, coarsely chopped
Juice from 2 lemons
1/3 cup extra-virgin olive oil
1/4 cup red wine vinegar
1 cup cold water
1/4 cup coarsely chopped fresh parsley
Salt and pepper, to taste

Makes 6 servings.

Preheat oven to 400° F.

Bake the potatoes for 1 hour or until they are tender when pierced with a fork. Remove from oven and cool to room temperature. Slice potatoes in half lengthwise. Using a spoon, scoop the pulp from each half into a large bowl.

Add the garlic and lemon juice to the potato pulp. Using an electric mixer, beat the mixture until almost smooth. Mixing on low speed, slowly add the olive oil and vinegar, alternating between the two. Add the water and mix by hand until smooth. Add the parsley and season with salt and pepper; mix well. Serve at room temperature.

hummus

MIDDLE EASTERN CHICK-PEA *and* GARLIC PURÉE

Spiked with garlic, this Middle Eastern appetizer traditionally is served with flat bread, pita bread, or crackers. Paired with olives, *dolmas*, fresh tomatoes, and thinly sliced sweet onions or cucumbers, *hummus* makes a perfect light lunch or summer dinner. You may use canned, cooked chick-peas (also called garbanzo beans) if you are pressed for time.

1 cup sorted and washed chick-peas
  (3 cups cooked)
1/2 cup *tahini* (Middle Eastern sesame
  paste)
10 cloves garlic, coarsely chopped
1 cup olive oil
1/2 cup fresh lemon juice
Salt and pepper, to taste
1/2 cup coarsely chopped fresh parsley,
  for garnish

Makes 6 to 8 servings.

Soak the chick-peas in 6 cups of water overnight. Drain and transfer to a large pot. Add 6 cups of fresh water and bring to a boil over high heat. Reduce the heat to moderately low and simmer for 1 1/2 hours or until very soft. Drain well.

Place the chick-peas, *tahini*, garlic, olive oil, and lemon juice in a blender or food processor. Purée until smooth. Season generously with salt and pepper. Serve in a bowl, garnished with chopped parsley.

crostini

WITH ARUGULA, TOMATO, *and* ROASTED GARLIC

Crostini, Italian for "small toasted breads," can be simply brushed with fruity olive oil and served as is, or capped with tasty and colorful ingredients, as in this version. The colors of the Italian flag are represented in this rustic appetizer, making this an appropriate starter for any Italian meal.

3 heads roasted garlic (see page 13)
1 loaf Italian or French bread, sliced into
   1-inch-thick rounds (about 24 slices)
1 1/3 cups extra-virgin olive oil
6 cloves garlic, minced
1 bunch arugula, trimmed and stemmed
   (about 24 leaves)
5 Roma (plum) tomatoes, cut into 1/4-
   inch-thick slices (about 24 slices)
Freshly cracked black pepper, to taste

Makes about 6 servings.

Preheat oven to 350° F.

Squeeze the roasted garlic pulp from the heads into a small bowl, taking care to remove any bits of skin from the pulp. Set aside until needed.

Arrange the bread rounds in a single layer on a baking sheet. In a small bowl, combine the olive oil and minced garlic and generously brush the top of each slice of bread with the mixture. Bake for 10 to 12 minutes or until the bread just begins to turn a very light golden brown. Remove from the oven and cool.

Cover each slice of bread with a leaf of arugula; top with some of the roasted garlic and a slice of tomato. Dust with freshly cracked black pepper, and serve at once.

roasted garlic spread

WITH CURRANTS *and* TOASTED ALMONDS

This rich cream cheese spread takes on a sweet tone from the addition of roasted garlic and currants. Spread onto crackers or bread for a simple hors d'oeuvre, or serve with raw vegetable pieces.

1/2 cup currants
1/3 cup brandy
3 heads roasted garlic (see page 13)
1 pound natural cream cheese (no gums
  or preservatives)
3/4 cup toasted almonds, finely chopped

Makes 6 to 8 servings.

Preheat oven to 450° F.

In a medium bowl, macerate the currants in the brandy for 30 minutes. Drain well and return to the bowl.

Squeeze the roasted garlic pulp from the heads into a bowl, taking care to remove any bits of skin from the pulp. Add the roasted garlic to the currants, along with the cream cheese and almonds. Using an electric mixer, beat on low speed until all ingredients are thoroughly combined. Season with salt and pepper. Refrigerate for at least 2 hours before serving. Can be refrigerated up to 5 days.

SOUPS *and* SALADS

elephant garlic salad

with SPRING VEGETABLES

Elephant garlic, with its jumbo-sized cloves, is much milder than ordinary garlic and is delicious paired with bright spring vegetables and goat cheese.

1 head elephant garlic, cloves separated and halved (unpeeled)

2 cups dry white wine

1 pound asparagus, trimmed and cut on the diagonal into 1-inch pieces

1/2 pound sugar snap peas, trimmed

3 large tomatoes, cut into large dice

1 cup packed fresh basil leaves, cut into chiffonade

1/2 cup olive oil

1/4 cup orange juice

Salt and pepper, to taste

2 small bunches watercress, trimmed

1/3 pound goat cheese, crumbled

1 cup toasted pistachio nuts, coarsely chopped, for garnish

Makes 4 to 6 servings.

Place the garlic and wine in a heavy-bottomed saucepan and bring to a boil over high heat. Reduce the heat to moderate and poach for 25 to 30 minutes or until the garlic is soft, but not mushy. Drain, and cool to room temperature. Remove and discard the skins. Cut the cloves into slivers and set aside until needed.

Cook the asparagus and sugar peas in a pot of salted boiling water for 30 seconds. Drain, and refresh in ice water. Dry on paper towels and place in a bowl. Add the tomatoes, basil, olive oil, orange juice,

and the reserved garlic; mix gently. Season with salt and pepper.

Place the watercress on a large serving plate. Arrange the vegetable mixture over the greens and top with the goat cheese. Garnish with the pistachio nuts, and serve at cool room temperature.

Note: The flavor of this salad becomes more pronounced as it stands. If refrigerated overnight, the flavor of the garlic will increase considerably. If you wish to do this, prepare the vegetable mixture and refrigerate, but do not assemble the salad until just prior to serving it.

Considered by early herbalists as a remedy for bronchial maladies, this garlic cough syrup may be taken whenever needed: Slice 1 pound of garlic bulbs, place in a large pot and cover with 1 quart of cold water. Bring to a boil over high heat and cook until soft. Add 3 tablespoons each bruised fennel and caraway seeds. Cover and let stand for 12 hours before straining. To the strained liquid add an equal amount of vinegar; bring to a boil over high heat and add enough sugar to make a syrup. Take 2 to 3 tablespoons as needed.

---

three onion-garlic soup

with GARLIC–GORGONZOLA CROUTONS

The ultimate soup for lovers of the "stinking rose." Reminiscent of the classic French onion soup, this version combines flavorful ingredients that create a comforting and heartwarming meal.

Three Onion–Garlic Soup:
2 heads roasted garlic (see page 13)
3 large red onions, halved and cut
   into 1/2-inch wedges
2 large yellow onions, halved and
   cut into 1/2-inch wedges
2 large white onions, halved and cut
   into 1/2-inch wedges
1 head garlic, cloves separated and
   coarsely chopped
1/4 cup olive oil
3 tablespoons unsalted butter
2 cups port wine
2 teaspoons each dried rosemary, sage,
   and thyme
2 1/2 quarts beef stock or low-salt
   beef broth

1/2 cup tomato paste
Salt and pepper, to taste
1 cup coarsely chopped fresh parsley

Garlic–Gorgonzola Croutons:
Half of a small baguette
3/4 cup olive oil
6 cloves garlic, minced
Salt, to taste
1/2 pound imported Gorgonzola cheese

Makes 6 to 8 servings.

To make the Three Onion–Garlic Soup:
Squeeze the roasted garlic pulp from the heads into a small bowl, taking care to remove any bits of skin from the pulp. Set aside until needed.

In a very large, heavy-bottomed pot, sauté the red, yellow, and white onions, and the chopped garlic in the olive oil and butter over high heat for 10 minutes, stirring frequently. Add the port and the herbs and cook until the liquid evaporates, 7 to 8 minutes. Add the beef stock and the reserved roasted garlic; bring to a boil. Reduce the heat to moderate and cook, uncovered, for 30 to 40 minutes, stirring

In England, garlic became popular for medicinal purposes during the First World War, when it was favored as an antiseptic dressing for wounded soldiers at frontline casualty stations.

from time to time. Add the tomato paste and mix well. Season with salt and pepper. Keep hot.

To make the Garlic–Gorgonzola Croutons: Preheat oven to 350° F. Slice the bread into 1/4-inch-thick rounds. Arrange in a single layer on a baking sheet. Combine the olive oil and garlic in a small bowl. Generously brush the top of each slice of bread with the oil-garlic mixture and sprinkle lightly with salt. Bake for about 10 minutes or until the bread just turns light golden brown. Remove from oven and cool to room temperature. Spread each crouton with some of the Gorgonzola cheese; reserve.

Just before serving the soup, return the croutons to the oven and heat until the cheese just begins to melt, 1 to 2 minutes; remove from the oven. Stir the parsley into the soup. Ladle the hot soup into bowls and top each with 2 or 3 croutons. Serve immediately.

burmese five-ingredient salad

with FRIED GARLIC

This salad reflects the intricate and intriguing flavors of Burmese cuisine and will delight anyone who savors the intense aroma and taste of fried garlic. Follow this appetizer salad with a spicy coconut soup to make a light, Burmese-style meal. You can find most of the ingredients for this dish in any Asian grocery store.

Dressing:
1/4 cup fresh lime juice
2 tablespoons fish sauce (*nuoc cham*)
1 tablespoon soy sauce
1/2 cup finely chopped fresh cilantro

Salad:
3 cups vegetable oil, for frying
1 cup raw peanuts
1 cup raw shredded coconut
1/2 cup dried shrimp
1/2 cup raw sesame seeds
6-inch piece ginger root, peeled
  and finely chopped
1 head garlic, cloves separated and
  thinly sliced
4 large lettuce leaves, for lining plates

Makes 4 servings.

To make the dressing: Combine the ingredients in a large bowl, whisking to form a smooth mixture. Set aside at room temperature until needed.

To make the salad: Place the vegetable oil in a 4-quart (or larger) pot. Heat oil over high heat, taking care not to let the oil burn. When the oil is hot (350° to 375° F.), add the peanuts and fry for 2 to 3 minutes or until they are golden brown. Remove with a strainer and drain on paper towels.

Repeat the process for the coconut, shrimp, sesame seeds, ginger, and garlic, frying each ingredient *separately* and removing from the oil with a fine-meshed strainer. Fry the coconut for about 15 seconds or until golden brown; the shrimp for 1 minute; the sesame seeds for 30 seconds or until light golden brown; the ginger for 15 seconds; and the garlic for 10 seconds or until light golden brown.

Place the fried ingredients in separate piles on a serving platter. Drizzle with the dressing, toss with a fork, and serve atop lettuce leaves on individual plates.

Note: If you do not have a deep-fat frying thermometer, you can test the temperature of the oil by dropping a 1-inch cube of bread into it. If the bread browns in about 1 minute, the oil is right for frying, about 365° F.

When the plague of the 1700s hit Marseilles, France, four felons were released from prison to help bury the dead. Despite their exposure to deadly germs, the four convicts survived. Popular belief credited their good health to a daily consumption of garlic wine.

white bean and garlic salad

with ITALIAN HERBS

Smoked ham, crisp yellow bell peppers, and tender white beans make a colorful background for intense garlic and herb flavors in this salad. Presented on a bed of greens, this Italian-style dish is good for lunch, or for an appetizer if served in smaller portions.

1 1/2 cups Great Northern beans, sorted and washed

2 bay leaves

1 large red onion, cut into small dice

10 cloves garlic, finely chopped

3/4 cup extra-virgin olive oil

1 cup dry sherry wine

1/2 pound smoked ham, cut into small dice

1 small yellow or red bell pepper, seeded and cut into small dice

2 cups finely chopped fresh basil

2 teaspoons each chopped fresh rosemary, thyme, and oregano

1/3 cup balsamic vinegar

2 cloves garlic, minced

Salt and pepper, to taste

Makes 4 to 6 servings.

Soak the beans in 8 cups of water overnight. Drain and transfer to a large, heavy-bottomed pot. Add 8 cups of fresh water and the bay leaves; bring to a boil over high heat. Reduce the heat to moderate and cook, uncovered, for 50 minutes to 1 hour or until the beans are tender, but not mushy. Drain and place in a large serving bowl.

Meanwhile, in a sauté pan, sauté the onion and chopped garlic in 1/4 cup of the olive oil over high heat for 3 minutes, stirring frequently. Add the sherry and cook until the liquid evaporates, 7 to 8 minutes. Add to the beans along with the ham, yellow pepper, herbs, vinegar, minced garlic, and remaining olive oil; mix gently. Season with salt and pepper. Serve at room temperature.

roasted garlic-pumpkin soup

with HAZELNUTS

Pumpkin and winter squash soups are often made with cream, but roasted garlic makes this soup smooth and creamy and adds richness without the addition of so many extra calories. A garnish of toasted hazelnuts adds pleasing flavor and texture to this golden fall or winter soup.

2 heads roasted garlic (see page 13)
1 large onion, coarsely chopped
3 cloves garlic, coarsely chopped
1 tablespoon ground coriander
2 teaspoons allspice
3 tablespoons unsalted butter
3 tablespoons olive oil
1 cup dry sherry wine
4 cups cooked pumpkin or winter squash
  (see *Note*)
2 quarts light chicken stock or low-salt
  chicken broth
Salt and pepper, to taste
3/4 cup toasted hazelnuts, coarsely
  chopped, for garnish

Makes 6 to 8 servings.

Squeeze the roasted garlic pulp from the heads into a small bowl, taking care to remove any bits of skin from the pulp. Set aside until needed.

In a large, heavy-bottomed soup pot, sauté the onion, chopped garlic, and spices in the butter and olive oil over moderate heat for 5 minutes, stirring frequently. Add the sherry and cook until the liquid evaporates, about 10 minutes. Add the pumpkin, chicken stock, and reserved roasted garlic; mix well. Bring to a boil over high heat. Reduce the heat to moderate and cook, uncovered, for 25 to 30 minutes, stirring from time to time. Remove from the heat and cool slightly.

In batches, purée the soup in a blender

until very smooth. Return to the pot and bring to a boil over high heat. Reduce the heat to moderate and cook for 15 minutes. Season with salt and pepper. Ladle into bowls and serve, garnished with the toasted hazelnuts.

Note: To cook a small, 3- to 4-pound pumpkin or winter squash (Hubbard, acorn, buttercup, or butternut), using a very sharp knife, carefully cut the pumpkin or squash into quarters. Place, cut sides down, seeds and all, in a shallow baking dish. Cover with water and bake in a 400° F. oven for 45 to 50 minutes or until the flesh is tender; remove from oven. When cool enough to handle, scrape the seeds from the flesh, then gently scrape the skin from the flesh; if the skin is particularly thick, you may be able to scoop the flesh away from the skin.

Eaten straight from the ground, garlic is almost mild, with a flat, one-dimensional flavor. Curing and drying for one month after harvest allows time for the proper development of flavor. A fully cured head of garlic, dry to the center core, can be stored for months on end.

peruvian-style potatoes

with GARLIC–CHILI SAUCE

This rendition of one of Peru's favorite potato dishes incorporates Latin spices and fresh green beans to perk up the flavors of the other, subtler ingredients.

4 pounds small new potatoes, quartered
1 large onion, cut into small dice
15 cloves garlic, finely chopped
4 jalapeño peppers, stemmed and
  coarsely chopped
1 tablespoon ground coriander
2 teaspoons each ground cumin and
  fennel seed (see *Note*)
1/2 pound green beans, trimmed and
  cut into 1-inch pieces
1/3 cup olive oil
2 cups heavy cream
1/3 pound *queso fresco* or mild feta cheese,
  for garnish
2 hard-boiled eggs, peeled and coarsely
  chopped, for garnish
1/2 cup chopped fresh cilantro, for
  garnish

Makes 4 to 6 servings.

Garlic was buried in the tomb of Egyptian boy-Pharaoh Tutankhamen, to protect his soul and riches in the afterlife.

Cook the potatoes in a large pot of salted boiling water for 20 minutes or until tender. Drain well and place in a large, ovenproof bowl. Keep warm in a 325° F. oven while preparing the remaining ingredients.

Meanwhile, in a very large sauté pan, sauté the onion, garlic, jalapeño peppers, spices, and green beans in the olive oil over moderately high heat for 10 minutes, stirring frequently. Add the cream and cook over high heat, stirring constantly to prevent the cream from boiling over. Cook for 3 to 4 minutes or until the cream is thick enough to coat the back of a spoon.

Add the cream mixture to the potatoes and mix gently. Transfer the potato-cream mixture to a serving bowl. Serve hot, garnished with the cheese, eggs, and cilantro.

Note: Ground cumin and coriander are readily available, but you may have to grind your own fennel seeds in a spice or coffee grinder. If using a coffee grinder, be sure to clean it thoroughly after grinding spices. I recommend purchasing spices in their whole form and freshly grinding them for each recipe.

ENTRÉES

linguine with seafood

and GARLIC TWO WAYS

The ever-popular garlic, clam, and pasta combination is taken one step further in this recipe by incorporating other favorite shellfish, fresh chives, and garlic cooked not one, but two ways. Serve with a green salad and plenty of warm bread for an inviting seafood dinner.

3/4 cup olive oil

2 heads garlic, cloves separated and
  thinly sliced

1 large onion, cut into small dice

4 cloves garlic, minced

2 teaspoons each dried thyme and
  whole anise seeds

1 cup dry white wine

1 pound bay scallops, small muscles
  removed

3/4 pound medium prawns, shelled,
  tails removed

3/4 cup cooked crab meat

1/2 cup cooked clam meat

1 pound linguine pasta

1 cup chopped fresh chives

1/2 cup minced fresh parsley

Salt and pepper, to taste

Makes 6 servings.

In a small sauté pan, heat 2 tablespoons of the olive oil over moderate heat. When the oil is hot, but not smoking, add the sliced garlic and sauté over low heat for 3 to 4 minutes, stirring constantly, until the garlic turns light golden brown. Remove from the pan with a slotted spoon and set aside until needed.

In a very large sauté pan, sauté the onion, minced garlic, thyme, and anise seeds in 1/4 cup of the olive oil over moderate heat for 10 minutes, stirring frequently. Add the wine and cook until the liquid almost evaporates, about 5 minutes. Add the scallops and prawns and cook for 3 to 4 minutes or until they are opaque. Add

Seventeenth-century herbalist Nicholas Culpeper wrote in his famous
Complete Herbal (1653) that garlic "kills worms in children,
purges the head, helps lethargy, is a good preservative against
and remedy for any plague, and takes away skin spots."

the crab and clam meat and mix gently. Remove from the heat and set aside until the pasta is cooked.

Meanwhile, bring 6 quarts of salted water to a boil in a very large pot over high heat. Add the pasta and cook for 9 to 10 minutes or until the pasta is *al dente*.

Drain well and place in a very large serving bowl. Drizzle with the remaining 6 tablespoons olive oil. Add the seafood mixture, chives, and parsley; mix gently. Season with salt and pepper. Sprinkle with the reserved fried garlic, and serve immediately.

roast garlic-rosemary lamb tenderloin

Lamb tenderloin is one of the more costly cuts of meat, but its velvety texture, mild flavor, and handsome appearance are worth the few extra dollars. Serve these elegant medallions on a bed of greens, cooked white beans, or pasta.

10 cloves garlic, minced
2 tablespoons olive oil
1 tablespoon Dijon mustard
2 teaspoons minced fresh rosemary
1 teaspoon black pepper
Juice from 1 lemon
6 lamb tenderloins (about 1 1/2 pounds)
Rosemary sprigs, for garnish

Makes 4 servings.

Preheat oven to 450° F.

In a small bowl, combine the garlic, olive oil, mustard, minced rosemary, black pepper, and lemon juice; mix well.

Coat the lamb with the garlic mixture, taking care to press the mixture onto all sides. Place the tenderloins on a flat roasting rack set inside a lightly greased roasting pan. Roast for 7 to 8 minutes or until medium-rare. Remove from the oven and let stand at room temperature for 5 minutes. Cut into 1/2-inch slices. Serve on warm plates, garnished with the rosemary sprigs.

garlic-fennel pizza

with TWO CHEESES

Garlic and fennel make an outstanding flavor combination and, when paired with the light smoky taste of domestic provolone and imported fontina cheeses, make an unforgettable pizza.

Fennel-Seed Dough:

1 1/2 cups all-purpose flour

1 1/2 cups bread flour

1 1/2 tablespoons fennel seeds

2 teaspoons salt

1 package active dry yeast (2 1/4 teaspoons)

1 cup warm water (110° to 115° F.)

5 tablespoons extra-virgin olive oil

Topping:

4 bulbs fennel, fibrous outer leaves discarded, trimmed, and sliced into 1/2-inch pieces

3 heads garlic, cloves separated and thinly sliced

1/2 cup olive oil

Salt and pepper, to taste

1/2 pound domestic provolone cheese, grated

1/2 pound Italian or Danish fontina cheese, grated

1/3 cup minced fresh thyme

Makes 2, 12-inch pizzas

To make the dough: In a large bowl, combine the flours, fennel seeds, and salt; mix well. In a small bowl, mix the yeast into the warm water, stirring until completely dissolved. Add the oil and mix well. Mixing with your hands, add the yeast mixture to the dry ingredients. Gather the dough into a ball and turn out onto a lightly floured surface. If the dough is too wet and sticky, add a little more flour; if the dough is too dry, add just enough warm water to form the dough into a ball.

Knead the dough for 5 minutes or until the dough is smooth and elastic. Place in a lightly greased bowl and cover with plastic wrap. Set in a warm place for 1 1/2 to 2 hours or until doubled in size. (A gas oven with a pilot light is perfect.)

Remove dough from bowl, punch down, and knead on a lightly floured surface for 2 to 3 minutes. Divide into 2 equal balls and cover lightly with plastic wrap. Let the dough rest at warm room temperature for 40 to 45 minutes, or until the dough no longer springs back when poked with a finger.

Preheat oven to 500° F. Roll each ball into a 1/4-inch-thick circle about 12 inches in diameter. Thirty minutes before baking the pizza, place two pizza stones in the oven to preheat. If you don't have pizza stones, use baking sheets and preheat in the oven for 10 minutes.

For the topping: In a large, nonstick sauté pan, sauté the fennel and garlic in the olive oil over high heat for 5 minutes,

stirring constantly. Season with salt and pepper and remove from the heat. Set aside until needed.

Bake the pizza dough blind (without the topping) on the preheated pizza stones or baking sheets for 5 minutes or until the crust just begins to turn golden brown. (If there are air bubbles, just pat them down with the back of a spoon.) Divide the fennel-garlic mixture between the 2 crusts; spread evenly over the top of each crust. Evenly distribute the cheeses over the 2 pizzas. Bake for 5 minutes or until the cheeses are *just* melted. Do not overbake or the cheeses will be rubbery. Sprinkle with the thyme. Cut into wedges, and serve immediately.

thai sweet-hot duck

WITH GARLIC *and* MINT

Typical of Southeast Asian cuisine, this dish combines sour, sweet, hot, and salty ingredients to create a round and balanced flavor. Specialty butcher shops, gourmet food stores, and wild game and poultry outlets often sell Peking, Long Island, Muscovy, or Barbarie duck breasts. If your butcher sells only the whole duck, ask them to remove the breast portion for this recipe. If you cannot find duck, substitute chicken breasts. However, the duck is sensational and lends itself to the tart and hot flavors of the other ingredients.

3 boneless duck breast halves, skin on
  (about 1 1/2 pounds)
1 teaspoon peanut oil
1 cup chicken stock or low-salt
  chicken broth
2 teaspoons light corn syrup
1 teaspoon ground star anise
4 to 5 Serrano chilies, stemmed,
  seeded, and thinly sliced
10 cloves garlic, thinly sliced
3 tablespoons fresh lime juice
2 tablespoons fish sauce (*nuoc cham*)
Lettuce, for lining a platter
1 cup chopped fresh mint

Makes 4 servings.

In a nonstick sauté pan, brown the skin sides of the duck breasts in the oil over moderate heat for 3 minutes. Add the chicken stock, corn syrup, star anise, chilies, garlic, lime juice, and fish sauce. Cook over moderate heat for 5 to 7 minutes or until the sauce is slightly thick and the duck is still pink in the center.

Remove the duck, leaving the sauce in the pan over very low heat. Place the duck on a cutting surface and let stand at room temperature for 5 minutes before slicing. Slice the breasts on the diagonal into thin slices. Lay the lettuce leaves on a serving platter, and place the sliced duck on top of the lettuce. Mix the mint into the sauce. Drizzle over the duck, and serve at once.

pasta puttanesca

This is an ideal pasta dish for those who adore the robust and assertive flavors of Mediterranean food. Serve with rustic bread and more olive oil, for dipping, along with a hearty Chianti or Barolo wine. *Perciatelli* is a long, skinny pasta that resembles spaghetti but has a pinhole running through its center. If you cannot find this type of pasta, you may substitute spaghetti.

2 medium onions, halved and thinly sliced

12 cloves garlic, coarsely chopped

2 teaspoons each dried rosemary, thyme, oregano, and basil

3/4 cup extra-virgin olive oil

1 cup dry white wine

3 cups peeled, seeded, and chopped tomatoes

1 cup pitted oil-cured or Kalamata olives

2 tins (4 ounces) anchovy fillets, drained and minced

1/2 cup drained capers

1 pound *perciatelli* pasta

Black pepper, to taste

1/4 pound freshly grated Parmesan cheese

In a very large sauté pan, sauté the onion, garlic, and herbs in 1/4 cup of the olive oil over high heat for 5 minutes, stirring frequently. Add the wine and cook until the liquid evaporates, about 5 minutes. Add the tomatoes, olives, anchovies, capers, and remaining olive oil; mix well. Keep warm over very low heat until the pasta is cooked.

Meanwhile, bring 6 quarts of salted water to a boil in a very large pot over high heat. Add the pasta and cook for 12 to 14 minutes or until the pasta is *al dente*.

Drain and place in a very large serving bowl. Add the tomato-olive mixture and toss well. Season with black pepper, and serve with the grated Parmesan cheese.

Makes 6 servings.

pasta shells with smoked chicken

in GARLIC CREAM SAUCE

This pasta dish is the ultimate comfort food. Garlic and cream team up regularly in sauces and soups because their combined flavors are so balanced. Bright green broccoli and the subtle, smoky taste of the poultry add color and flavor and make this a winning meal. If you cannot find smoked chicken you may substitute smoked turkey.

1 pound small pasta shells (*conchigliette*)
4 cups broccoli flowerettes (about
  1 large head)
3 cups heavy cream
10 cloves garlic, coarsely chopped
2 teaspoons each dried thyme and whole
  fennel seeds
1/2 to 1 teaspoon hot pepper flakes
1 cup chopped reconstituted sun-dried
  tomatoes
2 cups coarsely chopped smoked chicken
  meat (about 1 pound)
Salt and pepper, to taste

Makes 6 to 8 servings.

Bring 6 quarts of salted water to a boil in a very large pot over high heat. Add the pasta and cook for 8 to 10 minutes or until the pasta is about 30 seconds from being done. Add the broccoli; mix well and cook 30 seconds longer. Drain the pasta and broccoli together in a colander. Transfer to a very large serving bowl and cover with a damp towel.

Meanwhile, place the cream, garlic, thyme, fennel, and hot pepper flakes in a large, shallow saucepan. Bring to a boil over high heat, stirring constantly to prevent the cream from boiling over. When the cream starts to thicken (about 8 minutes), add the sun-dried tomatoes and chicken. Continue to cook over high heat, stirring constantly. Remove from the heat when the cream is thick enough to coat the back of a spoon, about 2 to 3 minutes.

Add the cream sauce to the pasta and broccoli; mix well. Season with salt and pepper, and serve immediately.

Why is slowly cooked or roasted garlic so sweet? When cooked, garlic not only loses its pungent aroma and much of its intense flavor, but some of its molecules are actually converted into complex molecules that are approximately sixty times sweeter than those of table sugar.

oven-roasted prawns

WITH GARLIC *and* FETA CHEESE

The combination of fresh spinach, garlic, feta cheese, and succulent prawns is reminiscent of many favorite Greek dishes. This recipe is fast and simple to make and is good as an appetizer; if served with a Greek salad of sliced cucumbers, onions, tomatoes, and mint, it would make a pleasing lunch.

2 large heads garlic, cloves separated
  and peeled
1/2 cup olive oil
1 cup dry white wine
1 large bunch spinach, trimmed (about
  3 cups packed leaves)
1 pound jumbo prawns, peeled, tails
  left intact
1/2 cup coarsely chopped fresh parsley
2 teaspoons each chopped fresh rosemary
  and oregano
Juice from 1 lemon
1/2 pound feta cheese, crumbled

Makes 4 servings.

Preheat oven to 425° F.

In a small sauté pan, sauté the whole cloves of garlic in 1/4 cup of the olive oil over moderate heat for 5 minutes, stirring frequently. Add the white wine and continue cooking until the liquid has almost evaporated. Cool slightly.

Place the spinach in a baking dish large enough to accommodate the prawns in a single layer. Evenly distribute the garlic over the spinach. Add the prawns, parsley, herbs, lemon juice, and remaining 1/4 cup olive oil. Bake for 8 to 9 minutes or until the prawns are opaque all the way through. Do not overcook the prawns or they will be tough and dry. Remove from the oven and top with the feta cheese. Serve immediately.

roast whole snapper

WITH PEPPERS *and* FRIED GARLIC

This rustic dish draws inspiration from Spanish cuisine, which includes garlic as one of the major components of good cooking. Red, green, and yellow peppers, crunchy garlic, and tender, white fish form contrasts in both texture and color. This visually attractive and easily prepared dish is ideal for serving to company. Be sure to include crusty bread for soaking up the aromatic juices from the roasted fish and vegetables.

1 medium red onion, halved and cut into
  1/2-inch wedges
3 cloves garlic, minced
1 red bell pepper, seeded and thinly sliced
1 yellow bell pepper, seeded and
  thinly sliced
4 green jalapeño peppers, stemmed,
  seeded, and thinly sliced
10 tiny new potatoes (about 1 pound)
2 teaspoons each chopped fresh marjoram
  and thyme, black pepper, and kosher salt
1/2 cup plus 3 tablespoons olive oil
4-pound red snapper, cleaned, with head on
1/2 cup imported beer
1 head garlic, cloves separated and
  coarsely chopped
Fresh herb sprigs, for garnish

Makes 4 servings.

Preheat oven to 425° F.

In a large bowl, combine the onion, minced garlic, peppers, potatoes, herbs, black pepper, salt, and 1/2 cup of the olive oil; mix well.

The exact number of true horticultural varieties of garlic in existence worldwide is unknown, but it is estimated at three hundred.

Transfer the vegetable mixture to a shallow baking dish large enough to accommodate the fish and the vegetables.

Place the fish on top of the vegetables and drizzle with the beer. Bake for 10 minutes. Remove from the oven, cover with foil, and bake for an additional 30 minutes. To check for doneness, remove a small piece of fish from the inside center; if the flesh is opaque, tender, and white, the fish is done. Do not overcook the fish or it will be dry and tough.

Approximately two-thirds of all domestically grown garlic is dehydrated and further processed into flakes, powders, and salts, or combined with other herbs and spices in a variety of blends.

but not smoking, add the chopped garlic and fry, stirring constantly, for 3 to 4 minutes or until the garlic just begins to turn light golden brown. Remove from the heat and set aside until needed.

Remove the fish from the oven and transfer to a heated platter. Spoon the vegetables and potatoes around the fish. Sprinkle with the reserved fried garlic, and garnish with the sprigs of fresh herbs. Serve immediately.

Meanwhile, in a small sauté pan, heat the remaining 3 tablespoons of olive oil over moderate heat. When the oil is hot

braised chicken

WITH WILD MUSHROOMS *and* WHOLE GARLIC

You may use any assortment of wild or cultivated mushrooms that is available, but be sure to remove any dirt, sand, pebbles, or grit from the caps and stems. Morels are one of the more expensive mushroom varieties, but if you can find them I would add four or five to the mushrooms listed in the recipe.

1/2 cup olive oil

3 1/2- to 4-pound chicken, cut into
  serving pieces, plus 2 legs

1 cup dry sherry wine

2 heads garlic, cloves separated and peeled

2 teaspoons each dried sage, rosemary,
  and thyme

2 cups chicken stock or low-salt
  chicken broth

1 pound fresh porcini (boletus)
  mushrooms, cut into thick slices

1/2 pound fresh shiitake mushrooms,
  stemmed and halved

1/4 pound fresh chanterelle mushrooms,
  halved if large

3 tablespoons unsalted butter

Salt and pepper, to taste

1/2 cup chopped fresh parsley, for garnish

Makes 4 to 6 servings.

Heat 5 tablespoons of the olive oil over moderate heat in a broad, heavy-bottomed pot large enough to accommodate all the chicken. Add the chicken and brown on all sides. Add the sherry, garlic, and herbs. Cook over high heat for 5 minutes. Add

53

the chicken stock and bring to a boil. Reduce the heat to moderate, cover, and cook for 30 minutes. Remove the cover and cook for an additional 15 minutes or until the chicken is very tender.

Meanwhile, heat the remaining 3 tablespoons olive oil in a large, nonstick sauté pan. When the oil is hot, but not smoking, add the porcini mushrooms and sauté over high heat for 2 to 3 minutes, stirring constantly. Add the shiitake and chanterelle mushrooms and the butter. Cook for 5 to 7 minutes, stirring frequently.

Add the mushrooms to the chicken mixture; mix gently. Season with salt and pepper and serve, garnished with the chopped parsley.

Transylvanians used garlic to keep vampires at bay, a belief that may have had some basis in science: "The touch of the vampire" was a dramatic synonym for diseases transmitted by mosquito bites, and recent scientific research has shown that garlic is actually an effective mosquito repellent.

roast chicken

with FIFTY CLOVES OF GARLIC

This classic dish, popularized by the late James Beard, helped elevate garlic to its present-day stature. There have been many recipes for chicken with forty cloves of garlic, but why stop at forty cloves when, in this case, more is better?

50 whole cloves unpeeled garlic
  (4 to 5 heads)
4- to 4 1/2-pound roasting chicken
2 sprigs fresh rosemary, or 1 tablespoon
  dried rosemary
Olive oil, for rubbing chicken
Black pepper, to taste
1 lemon, halved

Makes 4 servings.

Preheat oven to 450° F.

Place the cloves of garlic in a single layer in a lightly greased roasting pan. Roast for 20 minutes, stirring the cloves from time to time. Remove from the oven.

Pat the chicken dry inside and out with towels. Place the roasted garlic and the rosemary inside the cavity of the chicken. Truss the chicken, rub with olive oil, and sprinkle with black pepper. Place the

To make garlic-flavored olive oil, peel several cloves of garlic and add to a bottle of olive oil. Cover and let stand at cool room temperature for 1 month before using. The garlic flavor will become more pronounced with age. When used for dressings or for sautéing, the oil will impart a subtle and delicious garlic flavor to your foods.

chicken on a roasting rack set inside a lightly greased roasting pan; roast for 15 minutes. Reduce the heat to 375° F. and roast an additional 45 to 50 minutes. To test for doneness, turn the chicken upside down and prick the underside of the thigh with a fork; if the juices run clear, the chicken is done.

Remove the chicken from the oven and squeeze lemon juice over the skin. Let stand at room temperature for 10 minutes before carving. Serve with the roasted garlic from the inside of the chicken.

To make garlic vinegar, peel several cloves of garlic and add to a bottle of white or red wine vinegar. Cover and let stand for 3 to 4 weeks before using. The vinegar will improve with age, and the garlic flavor will become more pronounced.

daube of beef

WITH WHOLE GARLIC *and* ROOT VEGETABLES

An ideal fall or winter dish, this colorful, slightly smoky-tasting beef stew is made with seasonal root vegetables and whole cloves of garlic. Serve with buttered noodles, polenta, or rice.

1 pound bacon
2 pounds lean stew beef, cut into
 1-inch chunks
1 cup red wine
1 tablespoon each dried thyme and
 whole celery seeds
2 quarts beef stock or low-salt beef broth
1/4 cup tomato paste
2 heads garlic, cloves separated and peeled
2 turnips, peeled, halved, and cut
 into sixths
1/2 pound Brussels sprouts, trimmed
6 baby carrots, peeled and trimmed,
 or 2 carrots, cut on the diagonal into
 1-inch pieces
Salt and pepper, to taste
1/2 cup chopped fresh parsley, for garnish

Makes 4 to 6 servings.

In a large sauté pan, cook the bacon until crisp. Remove with a slotted spoon and drain on paper towels. When cool enough to handle, coarsely chop and set aside until needed. Transfer 1/4 cup of the bacon fat to a heavy-bottomed pot large enough to accommodate the meat and the vegetables.

Heat the bacon fat over moderately high heat. Add the beef and cook until brown on all sides, about 5 minutes. Add the red wine, thyme, and celery seeds and cook until the liquid evaporates, 3 to 4 minutes. Add 1 quart of the beef stock and bring to a boil. Reduce the heat to moderate and simmer, uncovered, for 45 minutes.

Stir in the tomato paste, garlic, and the remaining beef stock and cook 45 minutes. Add the turnips, Brussels sprouts, carrots, and reserved bacon; cover and cook until the vegetables are tender, 15 to 20 minutes. Season with salt and pepper, garnish with the chopped parsley, and serve.

According to the Talmud, *garlic serves many purposes: it seasons and preserves food, keeps the body warm, stimulates circulation, kills parasites and bacteria, satiates hunger, eliminates jealousy, and fosters love. The* Talmud *recommends eating garlic on Friday—the night devoted to conjugal love.*

chinese pork tenderloin

with GARLIC SAUCE

The first time I ordered this in a Hunan Chinese restaurant the surrounding diners stopped eating and began staring at the plate of food being served to me: tender slices of roast pork were concealed by mounds of sautéed fresh garlic—a fragrant and sensational meal! Serve this dish at room temperature with sautéed or stir-fried greens and steamed rice. You can find the ingredients for this recipe in any Asian market and in some natural food stores or grocery stores.

2-pound pork tenderloin, trimmed
   of any fat
2 tablespoons Asian sesame oil
1 tablespoon peanut oil
20 cloves garlic, finely chopped
1/4 cup dry sherry wine
3 tablespoons Chinese black vinegar or
   rice wine vinegar
2 tablespoons soy sauce
2 teaspoons Hunan-style salted black
   bean chili sauce
Sprigs of cilantro, for garnish

Makes 4 to 6 servings.

Preheat oven to 450° F.

Place the pork on a flat roasting rack set inside a lightly greased roasting pan. Roast for 15 to 17 minutes or until the center is still just barely pink. (The meat will continue cooking once it is removed from the oven.) Remove from oven and let stand for 10 minutes before slicing.

Meanwhile, make the garlic sauce: In a small sauté pan, heat the sesame and peanut oils over moderate heat. Add the garlic and sauté, stirring frequently, for 3 to 4 minutes or until the garlic just starts to turn light golden brown. Add the sherry and cook until it evaporates, about 2 minutes. Add the remaining ingredients except cilantro and cook for 1 to 2 minutes, stirring frequently.

Cut the pork into thin slices and arrange on a platter. Drizzle with the garlic sauce. Garnish with the cilantro, and serve immediately.

mexican pork-garlic stew

with HOMINY

You can find the ingredients for this dish in any Latin grocery store, and most major grocery stores carry some kind of *chorizo* sausage as well as canned hominy. Hominy is dried corn from which the hulls and germs have been removed through boiling, or soaking in lye. The corn has a unique and robust flavor and retains its shape in long-cooking stews and soups. Ground cumin and coriander are readily available, but you may have to grind your own fennel seeds in a spice or coffee grinder. If you use a coffee grinder, be sure to thoroughly clean it afterwards.

1/2 pound chorizo sausage, casings
  removed, crumbled (see *Note*)
1 large onion, cut into medium dice
14 cloves garlic, coarsely chopped
1/2 cup dry sherry wine
1/4 cup olive oil
3 pounds boneless pork shoulder or butt,
  cut into 1-inch pieces
1 tablespoon each ground cumin,
  coriander, and fennel seeds
2 teaspoons dried oregano
1 quart beef stock or low-salt beef broth
1 can (15 ounces) hominy, drained
  (about 2 cups)

Juice from 3 limes
1 cup finely chopped green onions
1 cup chopped fresh cilantro
Salt and pepper, to taste

Makes 6 servings.

In a large sauté pan, cook the *chorizo* over moderate heat until it loses its pink color, about 3 minutes. Remove with a slotted spoon to a bowl and reserve until needed. Sauté the onion and garlic in the *chorizo* fat (see *Note*) over moderate heat for 10 minutes. Add the sherry and cook until the liquid evaporates, 4 to 5 minutes. Add to the *chorizo* and set aside until needed.

Heat the olive oil in a heavy-bottomed pot large enough to accommodate all the pork. When the oil is hot, but not smoking, brown the pork on all sides in batches. Return the pork to the pot and add the *chorizo* mixture. Add the spices, oregano, and the beef stock. Bring to a boil over high heat, scraping the bottom of the pot to loosen any particles. Reduce the heat to moderate and cook for 2 hours or until the meat is tender. Add the hominy and lime juice and cook 10 minutes. Mix in the green onions and cilantro just before serving. Season with salt and pepper, and serve hot.

Note: Two types of *chorizo* are commonly available: Mexican and Spanish. I prefer the softer Mexican *chorizo* for this dish, but if you use the firm Spanish variety, slice the sausage into 1/4-inch pieces, and for the first step cook the same length of time as for the Mexican *chorizo*. Since the Spanish variety releases less fat than the Mexican, you will have to use 1/4 cup of additional olive oil for sautéing the onions and garlic.

SAUCES *and* CONDIMENTS

spiced garlic-tomato jam

Sweet, savory, and peppery ingredients add zing to this garlic-tomato spread. Yellow tomatoes lend it a warm and subtle color, but if you cannot find this variety, use ripe red tomatoes instead. Excellent with bread, crackers, or croutons or as a topping for pizza or sandwiches, this intense, slightly sweet spread should be served at room temperature.

2 cups water
2 cups Madeira, dry sherry or
  Marsala wine
1 tablespoon each fennel seeds, anise
  seeds, and pink peppercorns
1 large head elephant garlic, cloves
  separated and halved (unpeeled)
6 cloves garlic, quartered
1/4 cup olive oil
4 medium yellow tomatoes, peeled,
  seeded, and diced
1/4 cup chopped fresh basil leaves
Salt and pepper, to taste

Makes about 2 1/2 cups.

Place the water, Madeira, and spices in a large, heavy-bottomed saucepan. Bring to a boil over high heat and cook for 5 min-utes. Add the elephant garlic and return to a boil. Reduce the heat to moderate and poach for 35 to 40 minutes or until the garlic is very soft. Drain well and rinse the garlic in fresh water to remove all the seeds. Peel, and set aside until needed.

In a nonstick sauté pan, sauté the quartered garlic in the olive oil over high heat for 1 minute, stirring constantly. Add the tomatoes and the reserved elephant garlic. Cook over high heat for 5 minutes, stirring constantly, until soft and creamy and the elephant garlic has broken apart. Remove from the heat, add the basil, and then season with salt and pepper. The jam can be stored in a tightly sealed non-reactive container in the refrigerator for up to 1 week.

persian sugar-pickled garlic

I will never forget the first time I sampled pickled garlic. A Persian friend invited me for dinner, and as I walked through his front door that evening, I was enveloped in an overwhelming aroma of garlic, mixed with roast lamb. As I inhaled with ecstasy, he slipped a soft, almost sweet–tart bulb into my mouth. It turned out to be a clove of six-year-old pickled garlic. That evening we sampled garlic cloves that had been pickled for periods ranging from one year all the way up to twelve years. Since then, I have been making my own pickled garlic according to this recipe.

4 heads garlic, cloves separated, unpeeled
2 cups red wine vinegar
2 cups water
1 cup sugar
6 whole cloves (not garlic—the spice!)
2 tablespoons black peppercorns

Makes about 2 1/2 cups.

Place all of the ingredients in a large, heavy-bottomed saucepan. Bring to a boil over high heat and cook for 10 minutes, stirring from time to time. Reduce the heat to moderate and cook 5 minutes. Remove from the heat and cool to room temperature.

Transfer to a clean glass or ceramic jar large enough to accommodate the garlic and liquid. Tightly seal and refrigerate for at least 1 month before serving. The garlic improves with age for as long as 15 years.

salsa verde

ITALIAN GREEN SAUCE

This green herb sauce comes from the Emilia-Romagna region of northern Italy and is commonly served with roasted poultry. It also makes a fine pizza topping or sandwich spread, and it is excellent with grilled vegetables, meat, or fish.

2 cups coarsely chopped flat-leaf parsley
1 cup coarsely chopped basil leaves
1 tin (2 ounces) anchovy fillets, drained
  and coarsely chopped
8 large cloves garlic, coarsely chopped
4 tablespoons white wine vinegar
1/2 to 3/4 cup extra-virgin olive oil
Salt and pepper, to taste

Makes about 4 cups.

Place the parsley, basil, anchovies, garlic, and vinegar in a blender. Blend for 2 minutes, scraping down the sides of the container periodically. With the blender on low speed, slowly add the olive oil in a thin stream, adding a little at a time so that a smooth emulsion forms. When all the olive oil has been added, blend for 1 minute, or until the sauce is relatively smooth and emulsified. Season with salt and pepper. The sauce can be stored in a tightly sealed container in the refrigerator for up to 2 weeks.

roasted red pepper sauce

WITH FETA *and* GARLIC

Inspired by the popular Spanish *romesco* sauce, this spicy, red, and very garlicky sauce is terrific when used as a dip for vegetables, bread, or potatoes or as a sauce for grilled meats or poultry.

3 roasted red bell peppers, peeled, seeded,
  and coarsely chopped
1/2 cup toasted almonds, coarsely chopped
8 large cloves garlic, coarsely chopped
1 to 2 teaspoons red pepper flakes
1/2 cup olive oil
1/4 cup balsamic vinegar
1/3 pound feta cheese
Salt and pepper, to taste

Makes about 3 cups.

Place the red peppers, almonds, garlic, red pepper flakes, olive oil, and vinegar in a blender. Blend until smooth. Add the feta cheese and blend until smooth and incorporated. The sauce should be the consistency of thick tomato sauce. If the sauce is too thick, add a bit of water; if a tarter flavor is desired, add more vinegar. Season with salt and pepper. The sauce can be stored in a tightly sealed container in the refrigerator for up to 1 week.

garlic and sun-dried tomato pesto

The flavors of the Mediterranean come together in this straightforward sauce made from both fresh and dried tomatoes. I prefer sun-dried tomatoes in their dry form, rather than packed in oil, but either will be fine in this recipe. In the dry form they are considerably less expensive, as well as fat-free. Dried tomatoes can be reconstituted by soaking in hot water until soft and pliable, 20 to 35 minutes depending on how dry or how fresh they are. Drain them well before using in the recipe.

1 1/2 cups reconstituted sun-dried
   tomatoes, coarsely chopped
1 cup peeled, seeded, and coarsely
   chopped tomatoes
8 cloves garlic
1/2 cup olive oil
2 tablespoons balsamic vinegar
Salt and pepper, to taste

Makes about 2 1/2 cups.

Place the sun-dried tomatoes, fresh tomatoes, and garlic in a blender. Blend until smooth. With the blender on low speed, slowly add the olive oil in a thin stream, blending until a smooth emulsion forms. Slowly add the vinegar and blend for 1 minute. Season with salt and pepper. The pesto can be stored in a tightly sealed container in the refrigerator for up to 2 weeks.

INDEX

M

Mediterranean Garlic-Hot Pepper Olives 18
Mexican Pork-Garlic Stew with Hominy 61

N O

Oven-Roasted Prawns with Garlic and
    Feta Cheese 49

P

Pasta Puttanesca 46
Pasta Shells with Smoked Chicken in Garlic
    Cream Sauce 47
Persian Sugar-pickled Garlic 66
Peruvian-style Potatoes with Garlic-Chili
    Sauce 35

Q R

Roast Chicken with Fifty Cloves of Garlic 55
Roast Garlic-Rosemary Lamb Tenderloin 41
Roast Whole Snapper with Peppers and Fried
    Garlic 51
Roasted Garlic-Pumpkin Soup with Hazelnuts 33
Roasted Garlic Spread with Currants and Toasted
    Almonds 22
Roasted Red Pepper Sauce with Feta and
    Garlic 68

S

Sake-steamed with Garlic and Ginger 17
Salsa Verde (Italian Green Sauce) 67
Sauces and Condiments 63
Skordalia (Greek Garlic and Potato Pureé) 19
Soups and Salads 23
Spiced Garlic-Tomato Jam 65

T U V

Thai Sweet-Hot Duck with Garlic and Mint 44
Three Onion-Garlic Soup with Garlic-Gorganzola
    Croutons 27

W X Y Z

White Bean and Garlic Salad with Italian
    Herbs 31

CHRONICLE BOOKS

SAN FRANCISCO